The Adventures of Prince Panda – Learning ABC's

Jess Will

Copyright © Jess Will

"THE ADVENTURES OF PRINCE PANDA
- LEARNING ABC'S" 2020

All rights reserved. No part of this publication may be reproduced, distributed or conveyed without the permission of the author.

Hey princess, I just learned my abc's.
Oh really prince, that's great!
Do you know yours?
Of course I do.

Do you want to sing along together?

Sure is, so let's tap our knees and clap our hands.

Sure I do, learning is so much fun.

We should take turns too...

I'm ready when you are

You start and I will follow

So as soon as Princess said that, Prince started the beat.
He tapped his knees and clapped his hands.
(tap, tap, clap - tap, tap, clap) And said...

A IS FOR APPLE

B IS FOR BABY

C IS FOR CAT

D IS FOR DAISY

E IS FOR EAR

F IS FOR FAIR

G IS FOR GROW

H IS FOR HAIR

9

I IS FOR ICE BECAUSE I'M SO COOL

J IS FOR JOKE, JAM, JUMP OR FOR JEWELS

K IS FOR KITE

L IS FOR LIGHT

11

M IS FOR MICE

N IS FOR NIGHT

12

O IS FOR OX

P IS FOR POTS
PULL
PUNT
PITCH
AND PASS

Q

IS FOR QUEEN

R

IS FOR READ

S IS FOR STREAM   T IS FOR TEAM

PRINCE: YEAH! WE DO MAKE A PRETTY GOOD TEAM DON'T WE?!
PRINCESS: SURE DO, AND DO YOU KNOW WHAT'S NEXT?

U

IS FOR US WHEN WE YELL SO LOUD!

16

SO RUN AND TELL YOUR FRIENDS,
HOW MUCH FUN IT CAN BE...

WHEN A PRINCE AND PRINCESS
PANDA, LEARN THEIR ABC'S

No problem!
Thank you,
and let's do it again
That was fun!!
Thanks Prince!

THE END

CPSIA information can be obtained at www.ICGtesting.com
Printed in the USA
LVIW012144230920
666961LV00003B/29